1

Canoes went along the rivers.

This is a First People's canoe.
This canoe was made from a tree.

The people fished from the canoe.

Eels were in the water of the river. The First People ate eels.

Big fish were in the rivers. This is a Murray Cod.

The First People used spears to catch fish.

Canoes could go into small rivers.

The river sometimes went into the sea. There were fish in the water.

Rivers could be far away from the coast.

The rivers gave water, travel and food to the First People.

The First People could also walk along the waterway.

Word bank

animals

coast

sometimes

spears

Murray Cod

eels

canoes

people

rivers

along

fish

water

travel